# BEYOND MONETARY WEALTH

## Unlocking Hidden Gems in the Ever- growing Real Estate Market

By

Oscar Sylvan

Limit of Liability/Disclaimer of Warranty: This publication is designed to provide accurate and authoritative information in regard to the subject matter covered. It is sold with the understanding that neither the author nor the publisher is engaged in rendering legal, investment, accounting or

# Table of Contents

**BEYOND MONETARY WEALTH**

# Table of Contents

- Case Studies in DIY Wealth Building

## Chapter 5:
## The Power of Intellectual Capital in Real Estate
- Education as an Investment
-Market Analysis and Research: Non-Monetary Precursors to Success
- Developing Expertise and Monetizing Knowledge

## Chapter 6:
## Land Banking and Strategic Parcel Acquisition
- Identifying Undervalued Land Assets
- The Art of Land Banking: Holding for Future Returns
- Strategies for Accumulating Land Wealth

## Chapter 7:
## Non-Financial Leverage: Branding and Community Engagement
- Establishing a Recognizable Real Estate Brand
- Community Integration and Investment
- Using Influence to Secure Valuable Real Estate Opportunities

## Chapter 8: Environmental and Social Impact on Real Estate
-Incorporating Sustainability and Social Responsibility
-Creating Value Through Eco-Friendly and Community-Centric Projects

# Introduction

In the world of real estate, the pursuit of wealth has traditionally been closely tied to the movement of cash. The familiar path to prosperity has involved substantial down payments, securing mortgages, and navigating the complexities of property ownership. However, as the real estate landscape continues to evolve, a paradigm shift is underway—one that challenges the conventional notions of wealth acquisition.

Welcome to a journey that takes you beyond the traditional boundaries of cash-centric wealth-building in real estate. In this book, we explore the innovative strategies and unconventional approaches that enable investors to amass substantial riches without solely relying on liquid assets. We delve into a realm where imagination, resourcefulness, and creativity play pivotal roles in unlocking the full potential of real estate investments.

As we embark on this exploration of non-cash wealth in real estate, it's essential to redefine our understanding of wealth itself. Traditionally, wealth has been measured in monetary terms—bank account balances, property valuations, and investment portfolios. However, this narrow view often fails to capture the broader spectrum of value that can be harnessed from real estate assets.

In this book, we challenge the conventional definition of wealth and introduce the concept of "holistic wealth." Holistic wealth encompasses not only financial gains but also the utilization of non-monetary resources, such as knowledge, relationships, sweat equity, and environmental impact. By embracing a multidimensional approach to wealth, you'll discover the vast opportunities that lie beyond the constraints of cash.

Throughout the chapters that follow, we'll dive deep into various strategies and principles that empower you to tap into non-cash resources for building real estate riches. From creative financing methods to strategic networking, from sweat equity investment to leveraging intellectual capital, we'll provide practical insights and real-world examples that showcase the potential of these innovative approaches.

Prepare to challenge your preconceptions, expand your horizons, and embark on a path that redefines the way you perceive and pursue wealth in the realm of real estate. As the landscape shifts and opportunities multiply, the time is ripe to embrace a new era of prosperity—one that goes beyond the green in your wallet and unlocks the full spectrum of assets that real estate has to offer.

# Chapter 1:

# The Foundations of Non-Cash Real Estate Wealth

In a world where traditional notions of wealth have often centered around monetary abundance, it's crucial to lay the groundwork for a paradigm shift that extends beyond conventional thinking. This chapter serves as a compass, guiding you through the foundational principles that underpin the concept of non-cash wealth in the context of real estate.

## Broadening the Concept of Wealth

As we embark on this journey to uncover the multifaceted nature of wealth, it's essential to expand our perspective beyond the narrow confines of money. Wealth, in its true essence, encompasses an array of valuable resources that extend far beyond dollar signs. We delve into the exploration of intellectual capital, relationships, time, knowledge, skills, and intangible assets that often go unrecognized.

The chapter invites you to challenge the common assumption that wealth is solely synonymous with financial accumulation. By embracing a broader understanding of wealth, you open yourself up to a world of possibilities, where non-cash assets become the building blocks of your real estate empire.

## The Power of Non-Monetary Assets

Non-monetary assets have long been overshadowed by the allure of liquid funds and immediate financial gains. However, within the realm of real estate, their potential is immense and largely untapped. We examine the various forms of non-monetary assets, from expertise and influence to sweat equity and community impact. By harnessing these resources strategically, you can amplify your real estate ventures and achieve outcomes that extend beyond the transactional.

Through illustrative examples and insights, you'll discover the transformative potential of these often overlooked assets. This chapter empowers you to identify and cultivate these resources, infusing them into your real estate pursuits to unlock value that goes far beyond mere numbers.

## Real Estate as a Vehicle for Wealth Generation

Real estate has long been revered as a wealth-building vehicle, but its true power lies in its adaptability to different resource profiles. Whether you possess abundant cash reserves or are rich in knowledge, relationships, or creativity, real estate can be tailored to align with your strengths. We explore how real estate's versatility accommodates various non-cash assets, giving rise to innovative investment models.

By understanding the nuances of real estate's capacity to generate wealth, you'll be equipped to strategically deploy your non-monetary assets. From joint ventures that pool intellectual capital to partnerships that leverage influence, you'll discover how these unconventional strategies can amplify your wealth-building endeavors.

As we navigate the chapters ahead, remember that your definition of wealth is evolving. The conventional boundaries are being redefined, and the power to shape your financial destiny is in your hands. With a solid foundation in place, you're poised to explore the intricacies of non-cash real estate wealth and harness its potential to create a truly holistic form of prosperity.

# Chapter 2:

# Creative Financing: Leveraging Non-Cash Resources

In the realm of real estate, financial innovation extends beyond traditional avenues of cash transactions. This chapter delves into the realm of creative financing, showcasing the power of leveraging non-cash resources to secure and propel real estate investments. As we explore alternative financing methods, we'll uncover the transformative potential of barter, trade, joint ventures, and partnerships in the pursuit of wealth.

## Exploring Alternative Financing Methods

The landscape of real estate investment is no longer confined to the boundaries of cash-on-hand. Alternative financing methods offer a gateway to resourceful individuals who possess valuable non-monetary assets. From intellectual property and services to equipment and commodities, a wealth of non-cash resources can be utilized to fund real estate projects. We'll explore the feasibility, benefits, and challenges associated with these methods, equipping you with a diverse toolkit to navigate the evolving financial landscape.

## Barter and Trade in Real Estate

Barter, the age-old practice of exchanging goods and services, is experiencing a modern revival within the context of real estate. As the boundaries between traditional financial transactions and resource-based exchanges blur, innovative investors are leveraging barter and trade to unlock new opportunities. This chapter delves into the dynamics of property exchanges, skill-based negotiations, and the art of creating win-win scenarios through non-cash transactions. Through real-world case studies, you'll witness the symbiotic relationship between real estate assets and non-monetary resources.

## Joint Ventures and Partnerships for Resourceful Investors

Collaboration is a cornerstone of success in the world of real estate, and joint ventures and partnerships offer a unique avenue for resourceful investors to pool their strengths. This section explores the art of forging strategic alliances, where non-cash assets such as expertise, networks, and influence become invaluable contributions. From co-investing in developments to partnering on income-generating properties, you'll uncover the nuances of leveraging shared resources to achieve remarkable returns. Practical insights and best practices will guide you toward establishing synergistic relationships that transcend traditional financing models.

As you navigate the creative financing landscape, remember that your wealth extends beyond monetary boundaries. By embracing non-cash resources as viable and potent forms of currency, you're positioning yourself at the forefront of a new era in real estate investment. The principles explored in this chapter lay the groundwork for the dynamic strategies that lie ahead, as we continue our journey toward mastering wealth without cash in the realm of real estate.

# Chapter 3:

# Strategic Networking and Relationship Capital

In the intricate tapestry of real estate, relationships are the threads that weave success and prosperity. This chapter illuminates the significance of strategic networking and relationship capital as pivotal assets for achieving wealth beyond cash. As we explore the art of building valuable networks, leveraging relationships, and pooling resources through syndication, you'll uncover the power of collaboration and connection in the realm of real estate.

## Building a Network of Value

Networking transcends the mere exchange of business cards; it's a dynamic process of cultivating mutually beneficial connections. The foundation of your real estate success is built upon the network you create. From industry peers and mentors to potential partners and clients, your network serves as an invaluable repository of knowledge,

20

opportunities, and resources. This section guides you through the art of strategic networking, providing actionable steps for identifying key players, nurturing relationships, and harnessing the collective intelligence of your network.

## The Role of Relationships in Real Estate Success

In real estate, relationships are the currency that fosters trust, accelerates deal flow, and unlocks hidden opportunities. Discover how authentic connections can provide you with access to off-market deals, insider information, and collaborative ventures. We'll delve into the psychology of relationship-building, emphasizing the importance of integrity, reciprocity, and a long-term perspective. Through real-life anecdotes and proven strategies, you'll grasp the mechanics of converting relationship capital into tangible real estate gains.

## Syndication and Pooling Resources for Larger Gains

Pooling resources through syndication is a dynamic strategy that magnifies the impact of relationship capital. This section unveils the concept of syndication, where a group of investors collaboratively invest in real estate projects. By leveraging collective financial and non-cash assets, syndication enables resourceful investors to tackle larger and more lucrative endeavors. We'll explore the intricacies of syndication models, the legal and operational considerations, and the art of assembling a syndicate with complementary strengths.

As you journey through this chapter, remember that the value of relationship capital extends far beyond its immediate utility. Every connection you forge and every partnership you cultivate contributes to your reservoir of wealth. The principles elucidated here provide the foundation for creating a robust network, nurturing meaningful relationships, and unlocking the power of syndication. Embrace the understanding that the tapestry of real estate wealth is woven not only with financial threads but also through the intricate connections you foster along the way.

# Chapter 4:

## Sweat Equity and DIY Investment

The concept of wealth without cash extends to the sweat of your brow and the power of your skills. This chapter explores the realm of sweat equity and do-it-yourself (DIY) investment, where your time, effort, and expertise become valuable currencies in the pursuit of real estate success. As we delve into the realm of hands-on involvement, you'll uncover the rewards of investing your resources into your real estate ventures.

# Investing Time and Skill for Real Estate Returns

Sweat equity, the act of investing your time, energy, and skills into a project, is a powerful way to magnify your returns in the world of real estate. This section highlights the transformative potential of committing yourself to your investments. From property scouting and due diligence to property management and project oversight, every task you undertake contributes to the growth of your portfolio. By aligning your expertise with your real estate ventures, you not only enhance your returns but also gain a deeper understanding of the intricacies of the industry.

# Renovation and Improvements: Your Personal Investment

Renovation and improvement projects offer a canvas upon which you can paint your creative vision and expertise. By revitalizing properties through your personal touch, you elevate their value and subsequently increase your wealth. We'll delve into the strategies of identifying properties with potential, conceptualizing improvements, and executing renovations that align with your skill set.

As you embark on these projects, you'll realize how your sweat equity translates into tangible financial gains and appreciation.

## Case Studies in DIY Wealth Building

Real-world case studies serve as a testament to the potency of sweat equity and DIY investment. From investors who transformed fixer-uppers into profitable gems to those who applied their skills to manage properties effectively, these stories showcase the diverse ways non-cash resources can shape your real estate journey. These case studies provide insights into the challenges faced, the lessons learned, and the rewards reaped from investments fueled by personal involvement.

As you explore this chapter, remember that sweat equity isn't solely a means to an end—it's an investment in your growth as an investor and an expert in the real estate domain. By dedicating your time, knowledge, and skills, you're amplifying the value of your ventures and solidifying your position in the industry. The principles unraveling here offer a roadmap for aligning your passion with your portfolio, proving that wealth in real estate can be forged not only through monetary transactions but also through the dedication of your hands and heart.

# Chapter 5:

# The Power of Intellectual Capital in Real Estate

In the ever-evolving landscape of real estate, success is no longer solely reliant on financial investments and property acquisitions. A new dimension has emerged - the power of intellectual capital. This chapter explores how education, market analysis, research, and expertise contribute to achieving success in the realm of real estate.

## Education as an Investment

In the modern real estate industry, education has transcended its traditional role as a precursor to a career. It has evolved into an investment in itself. Individuals entering the field recognize that knowledge is not just power, but a pathway to profitability. Aspiring real estate professionals now understand the importance of learning not only the basics but also the intricacies of the market, finance, legalities, and trends.

Investing in real estate education, whether through formal degrees, online courses, workshops, or mentorships, equips individuals with the tools to navigate complexities. With a strong educational foundation, investors can make informed decisions, assess risks, and identify opportunities that might elude those without such insights.

# Market Analysis and Research: Non-Monetary Precursors to Success

In the world of real estate, accurate market analysis and in-depth research are non-monetary investments that yield substantial returns. Understanding the dynamics of a specific market, including supply and demand trends, demographics, economic indicators, and zoning regulations, empowers investors to strategically position their ventures.

Effective market analysis enables investors to forecast potential shifts and adapt their strategies accordingly. It acts as a compass, guiding them toward emerging neighborhoods, undervalued properties, and untapped niches. By cultivating a knack for research, investors gain a competitive edge, enabling them to predict trends before they become mainstream and identify hidden opportunities.

# Developing Expertise and Monetizing Knowledge

Expertise is the currency of the information age, and real estate is no exception. The accumulation of knowledge transforms individuals into authorities within the industry. This section delves into how one can develop expertise and, in turn, monetize that knowledge.

Becoming a recognized expert involves not only staying updated on industry trends but also contributing to the field. This can be achieved through publishing articles, giving talks, hosting webinars, or even creating educational content. By consistently sharing insights and offering valuable information, individuals can position themselves as go-to sources in a crowded marketplace.

Monetizing knowledge takes various forms, from consultancy services and advisory roles to creating educational products and platforms. Investors with a deep understanding of specific market niches can command a premium for their guidance. Additionally, the rise of online platforms provides opportunities to reach a global audience, expanding the potential reach of one's expertise.

Conclusion

In Chapter 5, we have explored the transformation of education from a prerequisite to an investment, the significance of market analysis and research in shaping successful strategies, and the process of developing expertise as a means of both personal growth and financial gain. In today's real estate landscape, intellectual capital stands as a formidable force, propelling those who harness its power to greater heights of achievement and prosperity.

# Chapter 6:

# Land Banking and Strategic Parcel Acquisition

In the realm of real estate investment, the concept of land banking and strategic parcel acquisition has emerged as a sophisticated approach to building long-term wealth. This chapter delves into the strategies and insights associated with identifying undervalued land assets, mastering the art of land banking, and implementing effective strategies to accumulate substantial land wealth.

## Identifying Undervalued Land Assets

Undervalued land assets are hidden gems in the real estate landscape, often overlooked by conventional investors fixated on developed properties. This section explores the methods and tools for identifying these assets, including:

**Market Analysis:**

Rigorous research and understanding of market trends can reveal pockets of undervalued land. Analyzing supply and demand dynamics, population growth, infrastructure development, and zoning changes can help identify areas with potential for appreciation.

**Location Scouting:**

Exploring emerging neighborhoods or areas undergoing revitalization can uncover undervalued land assets. Proximity to transportation hubs, amenities, and commercial centers can significantly impact land value over time.

**Zoning Insights:**

Understanding local zoning regulations and potential changes can unveil opportunities for land development or rezoning. An asset with underutilized zoning could be transformed into more valuable use.

# The Art of Land Banking: Holding for Future Returns

Land banking involves the strategic acquisition of land with the intention of holding it for future appreciation. This section delves into the principles and advantages of this approach:

**Patience and Timing:**

Land banking requires a long-term perspective. Investors must be patient, waiting for market conditions, infrastructure developments, or zoning changes that will drive land value upwards.

## Risk Mitigation:

Land is a tangible asset with intrinsic value. Even if market conditions fluctuate, its value does not plummet as drastically as developed properties during economic downturns.

## Strategic Positioning:

Investors can position themselves to benefit from urban expansion, demographic shifts, or evolving market demands. Holding well-located land can lead to substantial gains when the surrounding area develops.

# Strategies for Accumulating Land Wealth

Accumulating land wealth involves deliberate strategies that maximize returns and minimize risks. This section discusses various approaches:

## Diversification:

Acquiring land in different regions or with different potential uses diversifies risk and exposure to market fluctuations.

**Collaborative Ventures:**

Partnering with developers, municipalities, or other investors can pool resources and expertise to optimize land use and development.

**Value-Add Opportunities:**

Identifying opportunities to add value to acquired land, such as obtaining permits or entitlements, can expedite appreciation.

Conclusion

Chapter 6 has delved into the intricacies of land banking and strategic parcel acquisition. It has underscored the importance of recognizing undervalued land assets, the art of patiently holding for future returns, and implementing effective strategies for accumulating substantial land wealth. By mastering these principles, investors can navigate the dynamic real estate landscape and harness the power of land as a vehicle for long-term financial prosperity.

# Chapter 7:

## Non-Financial Leverage: Branding and Community Engagement

In the world of real estate, financial leverage is just one piece of the puzzle. Non-financial leverage, particularly through branding and community engagement, can play a crucial role in shaping a successful real estate venture. This chapter delves into three key aspects: Establishing a Recognizable Real Estate Brand, Community Integration and Investment, and Using Influence to Secure Valuable Real Estate Opportunities.

## Establishing a Recognizable Real Estate Brand

A strong brand can significantly enhance the value of a real estate project. Building a recognizable brand involves more than just creating a logo; it's about crafting a unique identity that resonates with your target audience. Here are some strategies to consider:

**Define Your Brand Identity:**

Start by clarifying your mission, values, and vision for your real estate projects. This foundation will guide your brand's messaging and design elements.

**Consistent Visual Identity:**

Develop a consistent visual identity that includes a well-designed logo, color palette, and typography. These elements should be applied consistently across all marketing materials and properties.

**Storytelling:**

Craft compelling narratives around your real estate projects. Share stories about the history of the property, the vision behind its development, and the positive impact it will have on the community.

**Online Presence:**

Establish a strong online presence through a well-designed website and active social media profiles. Engage with your audience through informative content, behind-the-scenes glimpses, and community-focused posts.

### Thought Leadership:

Position yourself as a thought leader in the real estate industry. Publish articles, give talks, and participate in relevant events to showcase your expertise and build credibility.

## Community Integration and Investment

Real estate projects don't exist in isolation; they are integral parts of the communities they inhabit. Demonstrating a genuine commitment to community well-being can enhance your brand's reputation and create long-lasting positive effects:

**Community Needs Assessment:** Before initiating a project, conduct a thorough assessment of the community's needs and aspirations. Tailor your project to address these needs, whether it's affordable housing, green spaces, or local businesses.

**Collaboration:** Collaborate with local organizations, businesses, and stakeholders to ensure your project aligns with the community's interests. This collaboration can lead to mutual benefits and a sense of shared ownership.

**Sustainable Development:** Prioritize sustainability in your projects. Implement eco-friendly practices, energy-efficient designs, and responsible construction methods that minimize environmental impact.

**Public Spaces:** Design projects with public spaces that encourage community interaction and engagement. Parks, plazas, and gathering spots can foster a sense of unity and pride.

# Using Influence to Secure Valuable Real Estate Opportunities

Influential connections can open doors to valuable real estate opportunities. Cultivating relationships within the industry and beyond can give you a competitive advantage:

**Networking:** Attend industry events, conferences, and workshops to meet key players in the real estate field. Foster genuine relationships by offering value and seeking opportunities to collaborate.

**Mentorship:** Seek out mentors who have successfully navigated the real estate landscape. Their guidance and insights can provide you with a wealth of knowledge and connections.

**Strategic Partnerships:** Collaborate with established players in the industry. Joint ventures, partnerships, and alliances can provide access to resources, expertise, and opportunities that might otherwise be inaccessible.

**Public Relations:** Leverage public relations to build your reputation and showcase your projects. Positive media coverage and a strong online presence can attract attention from potential partners and investors.

In conclusion, non-financial leverage through branding and community engagement can be as impactful as financial strategies in the world of real estate. A well-crafted brand, community integration, and strategic influence can elevate your projects, create lasting positive effects, and open doors to valuable opportunities. By focusing on these aspects, you can shape a real estate venture that not only thrives financially but also enriches the communities it serves.

# Chapter 8:

# Environmental and Social Impact on Real Estate

In recent years, the real estate industry has seen a growing emphasis on environmental and social impact. This chapter explores how real estate professionals can create positive change through sustainability, social responsibility, and community-centric projects. It also examines how these efforts can have broader effects, including wealth creation.

## Incorporating Sustainability and Social Responsibility

Real estate development can significantly impact the environment and local communities. Incorporating sustainability and social responsibility principles can mitigate negative effects and contribute to a better future:

**Environmental Considerations:** Prioritize eco-friendly designs, energy-efficient technologies, and sustainable materials. Implement green building standards such as LEED or BREEAM to reduce resource consumption and minimize carbon footprint.

**Reducing Waste:** Minimize construction and operational waste through proper planning and recycling initiatives. Embrace adaptive reuse to give existing structures new life and reduce the need for new construction.

**Responsible Sourcing:** Source materials from ethical suppliers who adhere to fair labor practices and environmental regulations. Support local businesses whenever possible to bolster the community economy.

**Energy Efficiency:** Incorporate renewable energy sources like solar panels and geothermal systems to reduce reliance on non-renewable resources and lower energy costs for occupants.

# Creating Value Through Eco-Friendly and Community-Centric Projects

Real estate projects that prioritize sustainability and community well-being can yield both financial returns and positive social impact:

**Value Creation:** Eco-friendly and socially responsible projects often appeal to a broader market and can command higher rents or property values. Forward-thinking buyers and tenants are increasingly seeking out sustainable properties.

**Community Engagement:** Involve local communities in the planning and development process. Gather input to ensure that projects meet community needs and enhance the overall quality of life.

**Mixed-Use Development:** Design mixed-use spaces that combine residential, commercial, and recreational elements. This fosters walkability, reduces commuting, and supports local businesses.

**Affordable Housing:** Prioritize the development of affordable housing units to address pressing housing shortages and promote inclusivity within the community.

## The Ripple Effects of Positive Impact on Wealth

Positive environmental and social impact can lead to a range of tangible and intangible benefits, including wealth creation and enhanced reputation:

Impact-driven projects can attract socially conscious investors who value sustainable and community-focused initiatives. This can lead to increased funding opportunities.

### Risk Mitigation:

Sustainable practices can reduce risks associated with changing regulations, resource scarcity, and climate-related events. A resilient project is better positioned for long-term success.

### Tenant and Buyer Appeal:

Forward-thinking tenants and buyers are more likely to be attracted to properties that align with their values. This demand can lead to higher occupancy rates and premium pricing.

### Reputation Enhancement:

A commitment to environmental and social impact enhances your reputation as a responsible developer. Positive public perception can attract partnerships, media attention, and favorable government policies.

In conclusion, the real estate industry has a profound role to play in promoting environmental sustainability and social responsibility. By prioritizing these aspects, real estate professionals can create value, positively impact communities, and generate ripple effects that extend beyond financial gains. Integrating sustainability and social responsibility into real estate projects is not only a responsible choice but also a strategic one that can yield lasting benefits for all stakeholders involved.

# Chapter 9:

# Negotiation and Persuasion: Currency Beyond Cash

Negotiation and persuasion are essential skills in the world of real estate. Beyond financial transactions, these skills play a critical role in securing deals, building relationships, and achieving successful outcomes. This chapter delves into the art of negotiation, the power of persuasion, and provides case studies that showcase successful non-cash negotiations.

## Mastering Negotiation Skills for Real Estate Success

Negotiation is a cornerstone of real estate dealings. Mastering negotiation skills can be the difference between a favorable deal and a missed opportunity:

**Preparation:**

Thoroughly research the property, market trends, and the parties involved. Understand your own needs and limits, as well as those of the other party

**Effective Communication:**

Clearly articulate your interests, goals, and expectations. Active listening holds equivalent significance in comprehending the viewpoint of the other party.

**Win-Win Approach:**

Strive for mutually beneficial solutions that address the interests of all parties. This approach builds trust and paves the way for future collaborations.

**Flexibility:**

Be prepared to adapt your strategy as negotiations unfold. Sometimes, unexpected opportunities arise from remaining open to alternative solutions.

# Persuasion and Influence in Deal-Making

Persuasion and influence are potent tools that can help sway decisions and foster cooperation in real estate negotiations:

**Building Rapport:**
Establish a positive rapport with the other party by finding common ground and demonstrating genuine interest in their needs.

**Highlighting Value:**
Emphasize the unique value propositions of your proposal. Explain how the deal aligns with the other party's goals and aspirations.

**Leveraging Social Proof:**
Showcase success stories and references to demonstrate your credibility and show that others have benefited from similar agreements.

Appeal to emotions by showing how the deal can fulfill aspirations or alleviate pain points. People often make decisions based on emotional resonance.

# Case Studies in Successful Non-Cash Negotiations

## Real-world examples of non-cash negotiations highlight the power of creative deal-making:

### Land for Infrastructure:

A developer offers land for the construction of a much-needed community center in exchange for streamlined permitting and other benefits from local authorities.

### Equity Swap:

Two developers exchange ownership stakes in separate projects to consolidate holdings in a prime location, creating synergy and enhancing overall project value.

### Historical Preservation:

A developer secures the rights to restore and maintain a historical building in exchange for tax incentives and prominent recognition within the community.

**Community Giveback:**

A developer commits to funding local education programs and green initiatives in exchange for community support and approval for a mixed-use development.

In conclusion, negotiation and persuasion skills are pivotal in the real estate industry. A mastery of these skills can transform negotiations into successful collaborations that extend beyond monetary transactions. By employing effective negotiation techniques, leveraging the power of persuasion, and studying case studies of creative non-cash negotiations, real estate professionals can achieve their objectives, build strong relationships, and create value that transcends financial considerations.

# Chapter 10

# Legacy and Long-Term Wealth Strategies

## Section 1: Beyond the Immediate: Creating a Lasting Real Estate Legacy

Creating a lasting real estate legacy requires careful planning and consideration. While immediate gains are important, focusing on long-term strategies can ensure that your real estate assets continue to benefit future generations.

**Diversification:**

Rather than putting all your real estate investments in one basket, consider diversifying across different types of properties and locations. This can mitigate risk and provide a stable foundation for your legacy.

**Multi-Generational Properties:**

Investing in properties that can accommodate multiple generations, such as family compounds or multi-unit buildings, can foster a sense of togetherness while providing ongoing rental income.

**Maintenance and Upkeep:**

Ensuring that your properties are well-maintained and updated over time will increase their value and desirability. A well-maintained property is more likely to appreciate and provide lasting returns.

**Philanthropic Initiatives:**
Incorporating philanthropic endeavors into your real estate legacy can leave a positive impact on your community. Consider endowing properties for charitable purposes or setting up scholarship funds.

# Passing Down Non-Monetary Assets to Future Generations

Legacy isn't solely about financial assets. Passing down non-monetary assets, such as knowledge, values, and experiences, can be just as valuable.

### Intergenerational Learning:

Create opportunities for knowledge transfer between generations. This could involve teaching property management skills, sharing stories about the acquisition and management of properties, or providing insight into real estate trends.

**Environmental Stewardship:**
If your real estate holdings include land or natural resources, teach your descendants about sustainable land management. Instilling a sense of environmental responsibility can contribute to a lasting legacy of conservation.

**Cultural and Historical Preservation:**
Properties with historical or cultural significance can be used to teach future generations about their heritage. Consider preserving the historical integrity of properties or sharing the stories behind them.

# Balancing Financial and Non-Financial Returns

A successful legacy involves more than just financial wealth. Striking a balance between financial returns and non-financial aspects can enrich your legacy.

**Family Unity:**

Real estate can be a tool for fostering family unity. Properties that encourage family gatherings or provide shared experiences can strengthen family bonds.

**Emotional Value:**
Some properties hold sentimental value beyond their monetary worth. Keep this in mind when making decisions about whether to retain or sell certain properties.

**Regular Assessment:**
Periodically evaluate the performance of your real estate assets, both financially and emotionally. Adjust your strategy as needed to ensure that your legacy remains aligned with your goals and values.

**Professional Guidance:**
Consulting financial advisors, estate planners, and legal experts can help you make informed decisions about the best ways to balance financial and non-financial aspects in your legacy planning.

Remember that creating a lasting legacy requires thoughtful consideration of both financial and non-financial factors. By incorporating these principles into your real estate legacy strategy, you can ensure that your assets contribute positively to the well-being of future generations.

**BEYOND MONETARY WEALTH**

# Conclusion

The journey through the world of real estate has shown us that wealth is not solely measured in monetary terms. Redefining wealth in the realm of real estate involves considering both financial and non-financial aspects, and understanding the enduring impact that properties can have on future generations. The traditional concept of wealth has expanded to encompass not only financial gains but also the preservation of knowledge, values, and experiences that can be passed down as a legacy.

As we've explored the strategies for creating a lasting real estate legacy, it's evident that the value of properties extends far beyond immediate profits. Diversification, multi-generational properties, maintenance, and philanthropic initiatives all play a role in shaping a legacy that stands the test of time. Beyond monetary returns, the ability to facilitate intergenerational learning, environmental stewardship, and cultural preservation underscores the importance of non-monetary assets in this legacy.

The evolution of non-cash asset strategies is a reflection of our changing understanding of prosperity. Intergenerational unity, emotional value, and a commitment to sustainability all contribute to the multi-dimensional tapestry of a meaningful legacy. By constantly assessing the performance of both financial and non-financial aspects, and seeking professional guidance, we can align our strategies with our values and aspirations.

In this age of redefining wealth, real estate emerges not only as an avenue for financial growth but also as a canvas on which to paint a legacy that transcends generations. The continued evolution of non-cash asset strategies reminds us that true wealth is a blend of financial security, shared experiences, and a lasting positive impact on the world around us. As we embark on our own real estate journeys, may we do so with a holistic view of wealth—one that leaves a legacy of prosperity, connection, and enduring value.